The Kids' Guide
to
Writing Great Thank-You Notes

The Kids' Guide
to
Writing Great Thank-You Notes

Jean Summers

THE WRITERS' COLLECTIVE™
Independent Books for Independent Readers

The Kids' Guide to Writing Great Thank-You Notes
© 2006 by Jean Summers

Interior Design: Barbara Hodge
Cover Design: Barbara Hodge

ISBN-13: 978-1-59411-125-9
ISBN-10: 1-59411-125-1

LCCN: 2005905654

Printed in the United States of America
10 9 8 7 6 5 4 3 2 1

Published by The Writers' Collective™ ♦ Cranston, Rhode Island

Dedication

For my parents who taught me
to write thank-you notes.

Acknowledgements

Thanks to my publisher, The Writers' Collective™.
To my editors, Bonnie Hearn Hill and Chris Gatchalian.
To my book designer, Barbara Hodge.
And to my kid authority, Marty Matthews.

Introduction

Congratulations!

You've just celebrated a birthday, graduated from school, or enjoyed a holiday like Christmas or Chanukah.

The good news? You got some cool gifts.

The bad news? Your mother says you have to write a thank-you note for each gift.

Uh-oh… you don't know how to do it. You don't want to do it.

Sorry, you have to do it!

But don't despair. A great thank-you note can be written in just a couple of minutes.

All About Thank-You Notes

Why write them?

Just because you get a gift, why do you have to write a thank-you note?

Because it will:

- **Show** respect and appreciation for the person who gave you a gift.
- **Make** other people as happy as the gift made you.
- **Build** the connection between you and the gift giver.
- **Help** you learn good manners.

Many people save every card and letter they receive. They treasure handwritten notes and letters as special links to friends and loved-ones.

Grandma and You

While you're busy ripping off all the wrapping paper, do you think about the time and effort that went into buying that gift and getting it to you?

For instance, what about your last birthday when grandma sent you the perfect gift? She went to a lot of trouble to do it.

Grandma:

- **Drove** to the mall and went to several stores and a card shop to find your present.
- **Wrapped** your gift in pretty paper.
- **Wrote** a message in the card.
- **Packaged** the gift and card for mailing.
- **Went** to the Post Office, waited in line to pay for postage, and then drove home.

Grandma took two hours to purchase, wrap, pack and mail your birthday present. Now it's your turn to thank her and let her know how much you appreciate her. How? Write her a great thank-you note.

Who gets one?

Do you need to send one to every person who gives you a gift? Most etiquette experts say every gift deserves a thank-you note. Others say if you open the gift in front of the gift giver and thank him or her in person you to not have to send a note. Your family can decide which advice to follow.

Remember: notes must be written for gifts that are mailed or delivered to you. Even if you phone the gift giver to say thanks you should also send a thank-you note.

When do you write them?

"The sooner the better," say etiquette experts.

How soon is that? No later than seven days after receiving a gift. After a week people will wonder if you received their gifts or value their efforts. If you've already missed the deadline don't panic. Even a late thank-you is appreciated. The important thing is to write a note as soon as you can. Remember the famous phrase: ***"Better late than never!"***

Why don't people write them?

There are five common excuses for not writing thank-you notes. Are any of these your favorite?

1. I don't know how. Oops — now you've got this book.
2. Writing is hard work. A great thank-you note can be written in only fifty words, or five or six short sentences.
3. I'm a poor writer. No one is going to correct your thank-you notes and send them back. If you ask your parents or a friend to read your notes and spot mistakes you can make corrections before mailing them.
4. It takes too long. If you write only ten words a minute you can write a great thank-you note in only five minutes. The next section will teach you how.
5. I don't feel like it! Do you always feel like going to school or brushing your teeth before bed? Sometimes we must do things whether we feel like it or not. Writing thank-you notes is one of them.

The good news

You don't have to write all your notes at one time. If you write two a day, you'll have written fourteen by the end of one week.

Five Quick Steps

Every thank-you note follows the same easy five steps. In the note that Bobby sent to his Aunt JoAnn (below) you can see these steps in action. Bobby wrote:

Dear Aunt JoAnn,

Thanks so much for the great birthday gift.

The Mariners baseball shirt is awesome! Ichiro is my favorite player. I'm going to wear my new shirt every time Dad and I go watch the M's play this season.

Thanks again for the cool birthday gift.

Love,
Bobby

Let's look at Bobby's note again. This time it's broken into the five quick steps.

Step 1 — Salutation:

Dear Aunt JoAnn,

Every thank-you note begins with the salutation—the written way of saying hello. The word "dear" is often used, but if that seems too old-fashioned, it's okay to use a more casual greeting like "Hi, Uncle Bob" or "Hello, Grandma Rose." Some people write the current date on the top of the note too, but that's optional.

Step 2 — First Thank-You:

Thanks so much for the great birthday gift.

Write a short sentence that thanks the giver. Mention the reason for the gift; perhaps it was your birthday. Use an adjective like "great" to describe it. If you're not sure what word to use, there's a list on pages 15 and 16.

Step 3 — The Details:

The Mariners baseball shirt is awesome! Ichiro is my favorite player. I'm going to wear my new shirt every time Dad and I go watch the M's play this season.

Describe the gift—in this case a baseball shirt. Say what makes it special and how you are going to use it. Two or three sentences will do. Go to page 17 for tips on ways to say why a gift is special to you.

Step 4 — Second Thank-You:

Thanks again for the cool birthday gift.

Write one sentence to thank the gift giver again.

Step 5 — Close & Signature:

Love, Bobby

Every note ends with an appropriate close. Many people close their notes with the word Love. You can also use Fondly, Warmly, Yours Truly, Sincerely, or even Best regards. Sign your name below the close and you're done. It took Bobby less than three minutes to write this note. Count the number of words — there are only fifty!

Ready to Write Your First Note?

If you need help you can use this fill-in-the blank form. It will guide you through your first thank-you note with HINTS to help you start and complete it. Use a pencil to fill in this form so you can erase it and use it again.

Step 1: Salutation

Dear _____,

Step 2: First Thank-You

Thank you for the _____ gift.
(HINT: pick an adjective from page 15 or 16.)

Step 3: The Details

I love the _____ because it

_____ .

(HINT: describe what makes this gift special; see a list of reasons on page 17.)

(and)

I am going to _____

_____ .

(HINT: describe how you will use the gift.)

Step 4: Second Thank-You

Thanks again for the _____ gift.

(HINT: repeat the adjective from Step 2 or pick one from the list on page 15 or 16.)

Step 5: The Close & Signature

_____ ,

(HINT: select Love, Fondly, Warmly, Yours truly, Sincerely, or Best regards.)

_____

(sign your name)

Congratulations—you've just written your first thank-you note. Now you can copy it onto a note card and mail it. Have more to write? Erase the words and fill in new ones. Pretty soon you won't need the form at all.

Tips for Writing Great Notes

You can describe every gift as a great gift, but there are many cool adjectives to use. Here are fifty favorites:

Adorable	Amazing
Astonishing	Awesome
Beautiful	Best
Breathtaking	Brilliant
Charming	Cool
Cute	Dazzling
Delightful	Excellent

Exceptional	Exciting
Extraordinary	Fantastic
Fine	Generous
Gorgeous	Grand
Impressive	Incredible
Lovely	Magical
Magnificent	Marvelous
Outstanding	Phenomenal
Remarkable	Sensational
Special	Spectacular
Splendid	Stunning
Stupendous	Super
Superb	Surprising
Sweet	Terrific
Thoughtful	Thrilling
Tremendous	Unbelievable
Unexpected	Unforgettable
Unusual	Wonderful

Weird gifts—what can you say?

Sometimes it's hard to figure out what to say about strange or unusual gifts. You can get around the problem by using words like surprising, unbelievable, unexpected, or unusual. You might say, "Thanks for the unique birthday gift," or "Thanks for the unforgettable graduation gift."

What makes a gift special?

If the gift is just right for you, say so. Gift givers love to hear that their present:

+ Is something you've wanted for a long time.
+ Makes you think about them.
+ Reminds you of a special occasion.
+ Is your favorite color.
+ Features your favorite singer or group.
+ Replaces something you've outgrown.
+ Is written by your favorite author.
+ Will help you buy something special or save for something you need.

Hand-made gifts

Did someone make a gift just for you? If so, let them know you appreciate the time and effort that went into making it. For instance, if your Aunt Sue knitted a sweater, you can say, "The sweater is beautiful. It must have taken you weeks and weeks to knit it! I love it, and I'll think of you whenever I wear it."

Money

There is a strange rule about money. Never mention the amount. Etiquette experts say you should refer to it as a "generous gift." For instance, do not say "Thanks for the forty dollars." Instead say "Thanks for the generous gift." Be sure to explain what you are going to do with the money. Will you save it, or use it to buy something special? It's good to be specific. You might say, "I'm saving for an iPod."

What about gifts you don't like?

Chances are you won't love every gift. It might be the wrong size, wrong color, or just plain wrong. Some gifts are stinkers!

No problem: just follow these three simple rules to write a polite thank-you note for gifts you don't like. First, don't say anything to hurt the gift giver's feelings; second, don't say too much; and third, find something nice to say.

You can hurt someone's feelings if you say:

- ◆ You don't like the gift.
- ◆ You wish it was something else.
- ◆ You hate the color.
- ◆ You can't fit into it.
- ◆ You plan to give it away or exchange it.
- ◆ You'll never use it.
- ◆ You already have it.

Susie hates orange-color clothes and never wears them. Unfortunately, her grandma sent her an orange sweater for her birthday. Here's Susie's gracious thank-you note for a gift she doesn't like:

Dear Grandma,

Thank you so much for the pretty birthday gift!

The teddy bear on the sweater looks like the one you gave me when I was a baby! It is very cute. And the sweater is warm and cuddly.

Thanks again for the nice gift.

Love,
Susie

Susie didn't mention the color. She found something nice to say about the teddy bear. And she didn't hurt her grandma's feelings by saying she isn't going to wear the sweater.

Sample Thank-you Notes

Dear Uncle Dave,

Thank you so much for the cool Christmas gift.

The new Jessica Simpson CD is just what I wanted! She is my favorite singer. I've already played it so many times Mom says I'm going to wear it out!

Thank you again for the awesome gift.

> Love,
> Maddie

Dear Bubby,

Thanks so much for your generous Bar Mitzvah gift!

I've been saving for a special new bike for a long time and now I'll be able to buy it. Mom said we can get it on Sunday. Dad is going to take a picture of me riding it so you can see how wonderful your present is.

Thank you again for a terrific gift.

> Love,
> Your happy grandson Mark

Dear Aunt Marcia,

Thank you so much for your great Chanukah present!

I wore the beautiful blue scarf and mittens to school yesterday. They are so warm and cuddly—and my favorite color, too! I'll think of you every time I wear them.

Thanks again for the cool gift.

Love,
Julie

Dear Grandma and Grandpa,

Thank you so much for the spectacular graduation gift.

I have wanted an iPod forever! I've already loaded my favorite CDs into it and listen to it all the time—even in bed at night.

Thanks again for the best graduation present anyone ever got.

Love,
Randy

Dear Aunt Helen and Uncle Tom,

Thank you for one of the best birthday gifts ever!

Two tickets to the best ballet in the world! I invited my best friend Wendy to go with me, because we've taken dance lessons together for years. We are both very excited about seeing the Nutcracker performed by professional dancers!

Thanks again for the spectacular gift!

Love,
April

Dear Andy,

Thank you for the awesome birthday present.

I was so happy to get the new <u>Harry Potter</u> book. Now I have the whole series! I've already started reading it and think it's the best ever!

Thanks again for the great gift.

Your friend,
Phillip

Dear Uncle George,

Thank you so much for the cool graduation present.

A new backpack is exactly what I needed! My old backpack fell apart over the summer and I didn't know what I was going to do about carrying all my books when I start High School this fall. Everyone says I'll have a lot of them! And this one is great — just the right size and color!

Thanks again for the thoughtful gift.

                         Love,
                         Bryan

Dear Carrie,

Thank you for the awesome birthday gift!

The tennis racquet charm is so cool! Where did you find it? I've already put it on my charm bracelet and it looks great. I'll think of you every time I wear it—especially at tennis camp this summer.

Thanks again for such a special gift.

                         Love,
                         Christine

Dear Mike,

Thank you for the super birthday gift.

I already loaded the NASCAR game on my computer. I played it a lot last night. It's great! I hope you can come over soon and play it with me.

Thanks again for the cool gift.

Your friend,
Teddy

Dear Ms. Magillis,

Thank you so much for the homemade fudge — it's delicious!

I was happy to jump in and look after Michael when your babysitter didn't come last weekend, but your present made me feel really special. I've already eaten half of it. How did you know chocolate is my favorite?

Thanks again for the totally great gift.

Sincerely,
Hannah Markham

Are thank-you notes just for gifts?

Not at all. You can send one to anyone who does something special for you. For instance you can write them when:

♦ Your best friend's family takes you skiing or to the beach for the day.

♦ Someone gives you tickets to attend a special ball game, movie or concert.

♦ Your neighbor feeds and walks your dog while you are on vacation.

Here's a note Joshua wrote to his neighbors after they included him in a trip to their beach cabin. It follows the five-step process.

Dear Mr. and Mrs. Jackson,

Thanks so much for taking me to the beach yesterday with your family.

I had a great time swimming with everyone and collecting sea shells. I'm going to put my shells in a glass jar and keep them on my desk where I can look at them when I do my homework.

Thanks again for including me in your family for such a fun day.

Sincerely,
Joshua

Get Ready to Write

You can write a lot of thank-you notes fast if you get organized first. You'll need to:

- Make a list of all the thank-you notes you need to write.
- Gather a few supplies.
- Make your list.

A list helps you make sure you send notes to everyone who gave you a gift. Let's look at Bobby's list. He received four gifts that require thank-you notes.

Bobby's Birthday Thank-you Note List

Gift giver: Grandma
Gift: Baseball glove
Date thank-you note mailed: April 10

Gift giver: Uncle Dave
Gift: CD—Justin Timberlake
Date thank-you note mailed: April 11

Gift giver: Aunt Sue
Gift: $40
Date thank-you note mailed: April 12

Gift giver: Aunt JoAnn
Gift: Seattle Mariners baseball shirt
Date thank-you note mailed: April 13

Here's a blank list you can use whenever you need to write thank-you notes. You can make photocopies to save to use for your next birthday or holiday celebration.

Occasion: _____

Gift giver:

Gift:

Date thank-you note mailed:

Occasion: _____

Gift giver:

Gift:

Date thank-you note mailed:

Occasion: _____

Gift giver:

Gift:

Date thank-you note mailed:

Supplies

Here are the supplies you need to gather before you begin to write. The last two items are optional. You only need them if you are going to decorate blank cards.

* Your completed Thank-You Note List (page 31).
* The address of each person on your list.
* A note card and envelope for each person on your Thank-You Note List.
* A first class stamp for each note.
* A pen or pencil.
* Markers, scissors, crayons, glue, glitters, stickers or other art supplies for decorating your cards.
* Photos of you with each gift.

Make it a party!

If it's hard for you to write your thank-you notes alone you can do it with a friend or your brothers and sisters. Make it a thank-you note writing party!

You can have a contest to see who finishes their notes first. And you can share ideas for decorating the cards and take photos of each other to include with your cards.

You can make cards or buy them by the box or individually.

Note Cards and Envelopes

What's on them is up to you. They can be blank or say Thank You! in big letters, or show a picture or design.

There are many great software packages that help you create one-of-a-kind cards, which you can buy for between $10 to $50, like *Hallmark Card Studio, Greeting Card Factory*, or *CreataCard* by American Greetings. You can even find free card creation software programs on the Net.

Select whatever size card works best for you. If you have large handwriting, bigger cards might be better.

Make your notes look special

You can personalize blank cards by drawing pictures or decorating them with stickers, marking pens, or rubber stamps.

Or you can be the star. Take a photo that shows you holding or wearing the new gift and glue the photo onto the front of the card.

Do you have to use note cards?

There's no rule that says you must use note cards. Some people like to use postcards and others like to use colorful paper.

What about handwriting?

Handwritten cards are considered the most personal. But, it's okay to type the words on a computer and print them out on blank card stock or pretty paper.

Where do you write on the card?

Write your note on the inside bottom portion of the card. If you run out of room, turn the card over and finish your note on the lower back.

What goes on the envelope?

An envelope has three areas that must be filled in before the card can be mailed: your address, the gift giver's address and a place for the postage stamp.

+ **Your address:** This goes in the upper left corner of the envelope and includes:
  + Your name
  + Your street address
  + Your City, State and Zip Code
  + USA

Only include "USA" if you're sending the note outside the USA.

- **Gift Giver's Address:** This goes in the middle of the envelope. Use the same format as above, but fill in the gift giver's information. If you are not sure about their zip code, you can look it up in your telephone book or online at www.usps.com/zip4. If they live in another country, add the country name as a fourth line after the zip code. Also, it's a good idea to print addresses. If the Postal Service can't read the address they can't deliver it.

- **Postage stamp:** This goes in the upper right corner. Most of the time you can use a first class stamp, but if the envelope is really big, or if it's going to another country you'll need to go to the Post Office to determine the correct amount of postage.

Place the card in the envelope

Be sure to insert your card in the envelope so the front is visible when the envelope is opened. This way the recipient can see right away that it's a special, thank-you card.

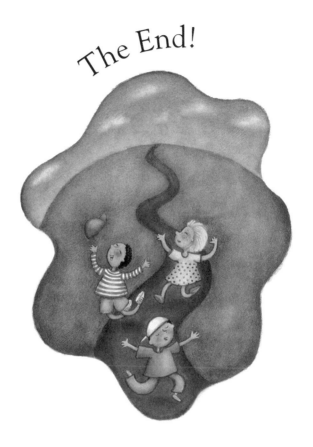

And now, congratulations! We're done! We've covered all the basics of how to write great thank-you notes. Now you're ready to write your own. Happy writing!

My Thank-You Notes

_____

_____

_____

_____

_____

_____

_____

_____

_____

_____

_____

_____

_____

_____

_____

My Thank-You Notes

_____

_____

_____

_____

_____

_____

_____

_____

_____

_____

_____

_____

_____

_____

_____

_____

My Thank-You Notes

_____

_____

_____

_____

_____

_____

_____

_____

_____

_____

_____

_____

_____

_____

_____

_____